CHURCH SIGNS

COLLECTOR'S EDITION

Publishing Company
Sock And Roll Corporation
900 20th Avenue South, Suite 614
Nashville, TN 37212

978-0-9789715-4-0

COLLECTOR'S EDITION

FEATURING MANY NEW INSPIRATIONAL SIGNS, AS WELL AS THE AUTHOR'S FAVORITES FROM HIS THREE PREVIOUSLY RELEASED VOLUMES. THIS COLLECTOR'S EDITION CELEBRATES THE FAITH, LOVE & LAUGHTER DISPLAYED EVERY DAY ACROSS AMERICA.

DEDICATION

To Mom and Dad who started the adventure.

To my wife, Maureen, and my son, William, who make the journey so sweet.

And to God who holds the maps.

FOREWORD

Church signs are part of the American cultural landscape. Like brilliant wildflowers or persistent weeds, church signs edge the borders of our highways, streets, and back roads. You'll see them almost anywhere — rising from Kentucky corn fields, shadowed by California palms, standing firm in Louisiana bogs, or even clinging to a stone wall on New York's Fifth Avenue. Americans may not wear their faith on their sleeves, but they love to show it on the road.

By "church signs" I don't mean the plain marquees that display Sunday's sermon schedule. Instead, I'm talking about those bold, often unruly-looking signboards that have slots for large black moveable type. The perfect template for dishing out a pithy sermon, like "Know God, no sin," or "Exercise daily, walk with the Lord." There's nothing static about these signs. They're meant to change, and they usually change weekly. Sometimes daily, if a gust of wind shakes loose a dangling "k," and what was once an intended "know" becomes an accidental or perhaps divinely inspired "now."

Church signs are meant to challenge as well as change. They confront their readers to live better lives, to love more deeply, to pray more often. And they're aimed at the kind of audience that every advertising executive dreams about — a captive one. It's hard to avert your eyes to these signs of faith. It's not like the car radio where you can flip the dial if you don't like what's on. Church signs act like powerful spiritual magnets, drawing you in for a closer look, for a sacred moment of reflection.

Or sometimes for just a laugh. Church signs are often one-liners, with the rhythm, timing, and delivery of a vaudeville performer. Puns are popular. "This church is prayer conditioned" comes to mind. Poking fun at the human condition is fair game too, as in "A sharp tongue and a dull mind are usually found in the same head." And, of course, like the bad stand-up comic who needs the hook, some signs are downright groaners, blessedly removed from public sight by the Monday morning commute.

Every sign tells its own story, revealing a rich variety of wisdom, wit, and faith. In some photos, the words say it all. In others, the message is in the details — like the beer truck in the background, the ominous desert sky, or the father and son in the doorway. Collectively, these church signs offer one great American sermon.

I hope you will enjoy this photographic journey of faith.

Donald Seitz

CONTENTS

FAITH

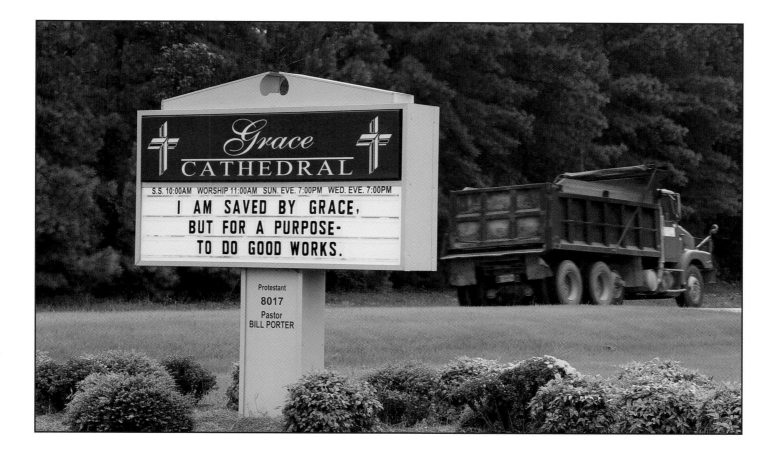

NAME THAT PASTOR

It must be comforting to know that your pastor has a name like Hope.

And if you keep a close eye on church signs across America, you'll run across hundreds of names that inspire and delight the imagination. In the scrub brush of Vega, Texas, you could have a Peach for a pastor; while in the steel canyons of Manhattan, you could build your church upon a rock – Pastor Rock, that is. Driving through the dizzying lights of Los Angeles, plan to attend bible study with Pastor Bright. And back in Waco you could share a church supper with a Goodfellow.

Would you feel uneasy passing the collection plate in Arizona when a Crook is standing in the pulpit? Or would a Kentucky Pastor named Grace ease your mind and loosen your wallet? By the way, Pastor Cruel in Georgia wants you to know that he isn't.

Expect to hear uplifting sermons in northern Michigan by Pastor Downer; while in the foothills of Tennessee, Pastor Broom will sweep away your cares.

And, oh yes, whether you're Baptist or Presbyterian, whether you prefer total immersion or a light sprinkling, who wouldn't want to witness a baptism by Pastor Dipper?

CEDAR BLUFF
BAPTIST CHURCH

Home Of
Go ⟶ Forth Missions

WAL-MART IS NOT
THE ONLY
SAVING PLACE
COME ON IN !

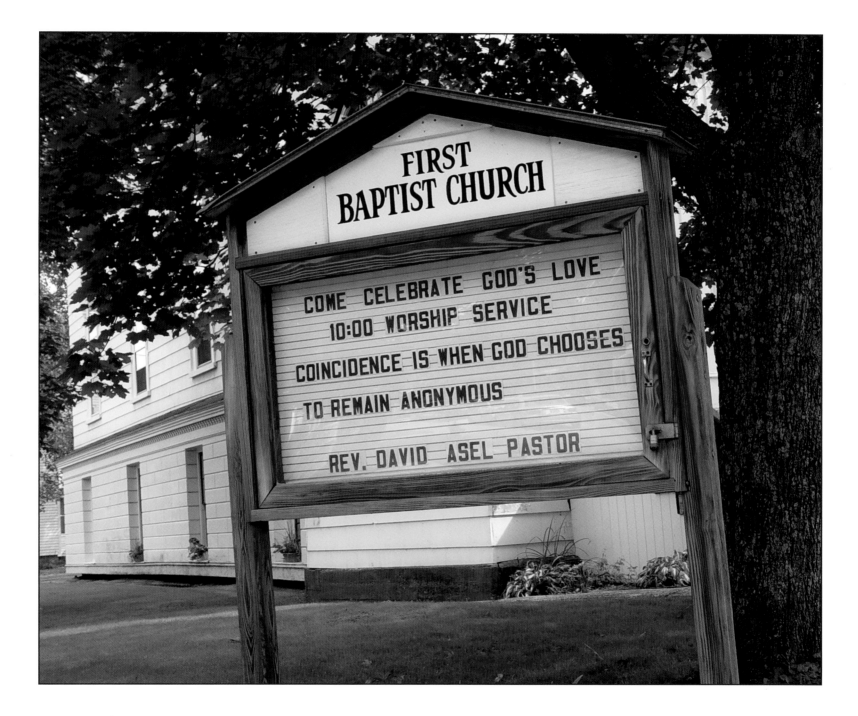

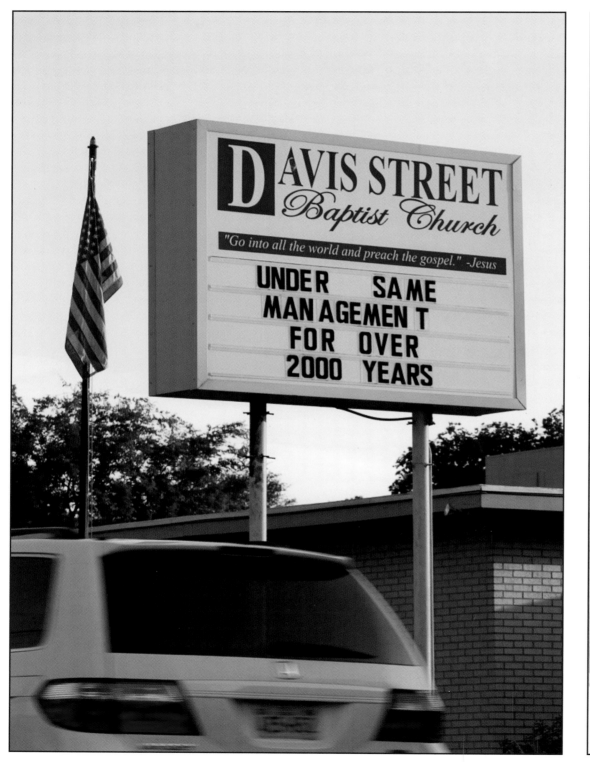

Church Sign Trivia Challenge

Two pastors of two churches separated by a lone country mile agreed to offer their community of Stillwater, Minnesota, a game of Church Sign Trivia. The pastor of Our Savior's Lutheran Church threw down the first challenge. His sign said:

NAME THE TEN COMMANDMENTS
IN NO PARTICULAR ORDER
--ANSWER IN ONE MILE

At the Bethany Evangelical Covenant Church, one mile to the southwest, drivers looked over to see:

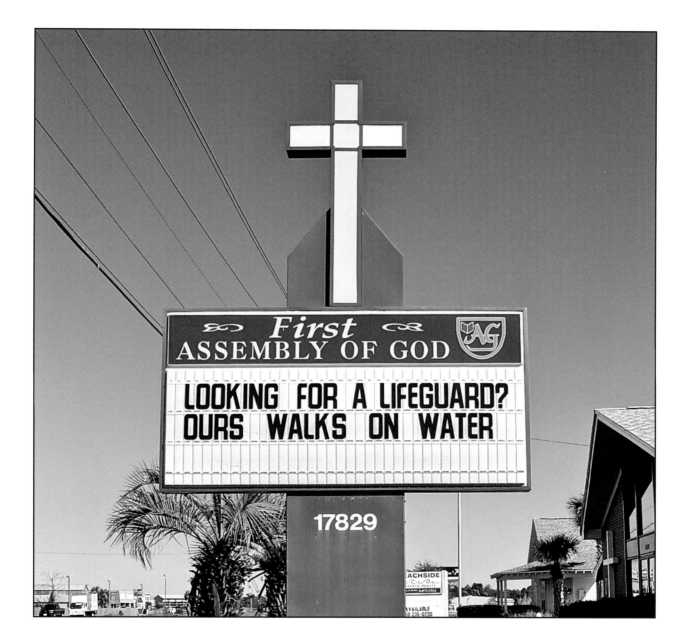

ADVICE

LESS IS MORE

If brevity is the soul of wit, it is also at the heart of faith – at least on the road. The average church sign is about seven words long.

There are several practical reasons for this. First, church signs need to be quick reads, understandable at a glance to drivers passing by. Second, words are not cheap. Or better said, large plastic letters are not cheap. A box of 6 inch letters will set back a small church on a limited budget more than two hundred bucks. Not to mention, broken and lost letters are always needing to be replaced. Third, space is a problem. The size of the sign and the size of the letters pretty much dictate that ten or more words will be a tight, illegible squeeze.

And as the following story suggests, some pastors are quick to learn that less is more when it comes to church signs.

A Primitive Church Tale Retold

Very early Sunday morning the pastor of Orchard Lake Church was rushing to change the sign out front. The new message proclaimed:

THE END IS NEAR!
TURN YOURSELF AROUND

The first person who drove by didn't appreciate the message, and he shouted back to the pastor, "Leave us alone, you religious nut!" A moment later, the pastor heard a loud splash. Realizing his words were misconstrued, the pastor quickly put up a new sign:

BRIDGE OUT AHEAD!

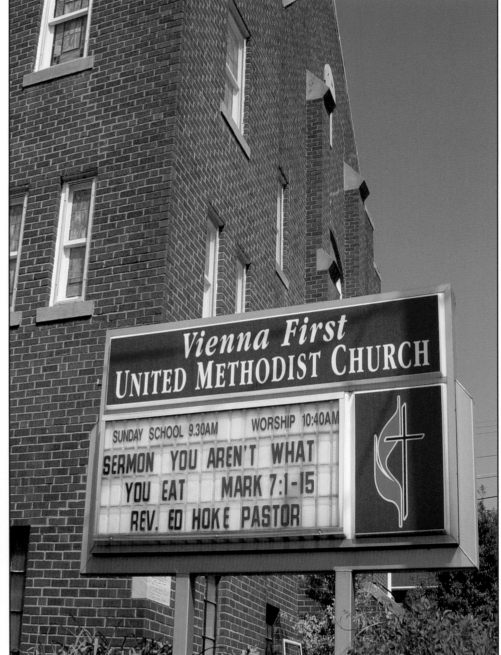

BACKGROUND CHECKS

One of the great delights of photographing church signs is to discover how often the background of the sign can enhance, inform and even transcend the message itself. On the opposite page is perhaps my favorite example of this – where the background and the message seem almost inextricably linked. You'll find other examples throughout the book, but one deserves special mention: a magnificent double-rainbow appeared while I was photographing a sign with the oft-repeated expression "Seven Days Without God Makes One Weak." Was this mere chance or divine timing? As I took in the beautiful sight, I was reminded of the "Coincidence" message that appears on p. 29.

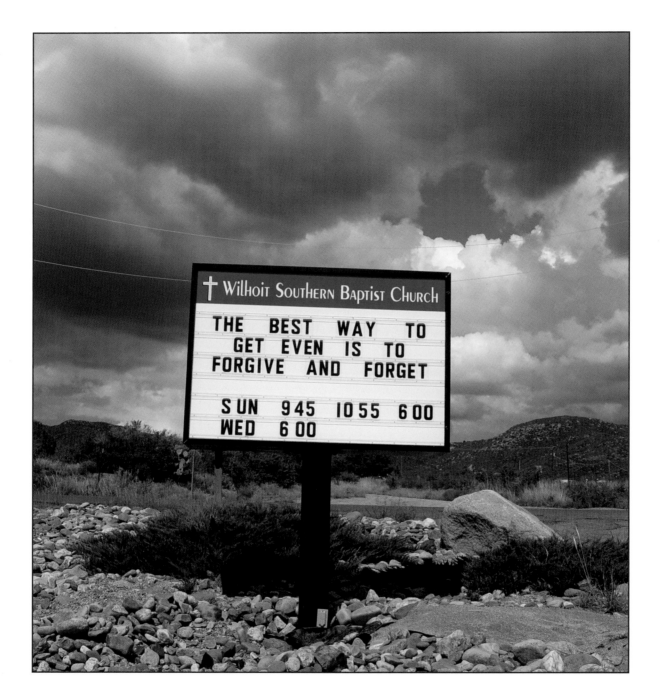

THE HEAVIEST THING
YOU CAN CARRY
IS A GRUDGE

THOSE WHO FOLLOW
THE CROWD ARE
QUICKLY LOST IN IT.

PRAYER

IF YOU WANT
A BETTER PREACHER
PRAY FOR THE ONE YOU GOT
CAN'T SLEEP? WE CAN HELP.
THE PASTOR'S SERMONS ARE
NOW AVAILABLE ON TAPE.

BUT SERIOUSLY, FOLKS…

The life of a pastor is serious business. Preaching the gospel, comforting the sick, inspiring the dispirited, and lifting the fallen. But as demanding as the occupation may be, many pastors — indeed, some of the most effective — have that unique gift of not taking themselves too seriously.

Nothing better illustrates this self-deprecating quality than the following church signs that were approved — remarkably — by the pastors themselves.

NOW'S A GOOD TIME TO VISIT OUR PASTOR'S ON VACATION

THE PASTOR SAW HIS SHADOW
SIX MORE WEEKS OF
LOUSY SERMONS

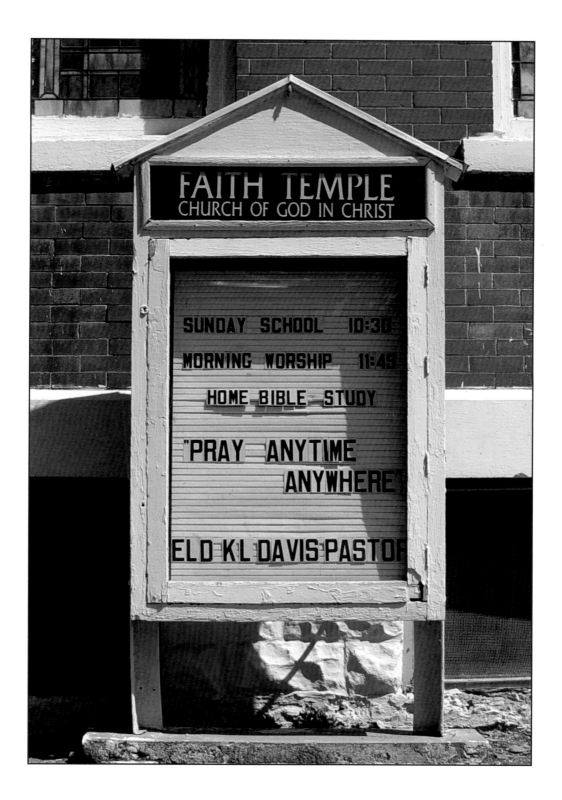

MADE IN HEAVEN

When I asked a pastor in Franklin, Tennessee, for his favorite church sign, he told me of the time he was counseling a young couple through a very rocky period in their marriage. During one rather heated session, when the husband and wife couldn't agree on anything, the wife turned to the pastor with great exasperation, "I thought you said marriage was made in Heaven!" The next morning the pastor put out a new church sign:

MARRIAGE WAS MADE IN HEAVEN
AND SO WAS THUNDER AND LIGHTNING!

LOVE &
LIGHT

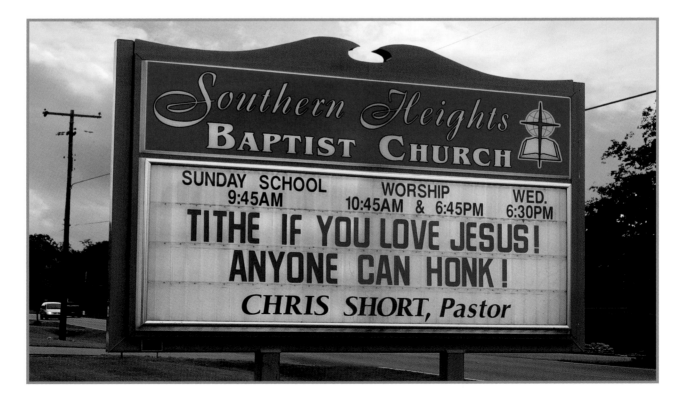

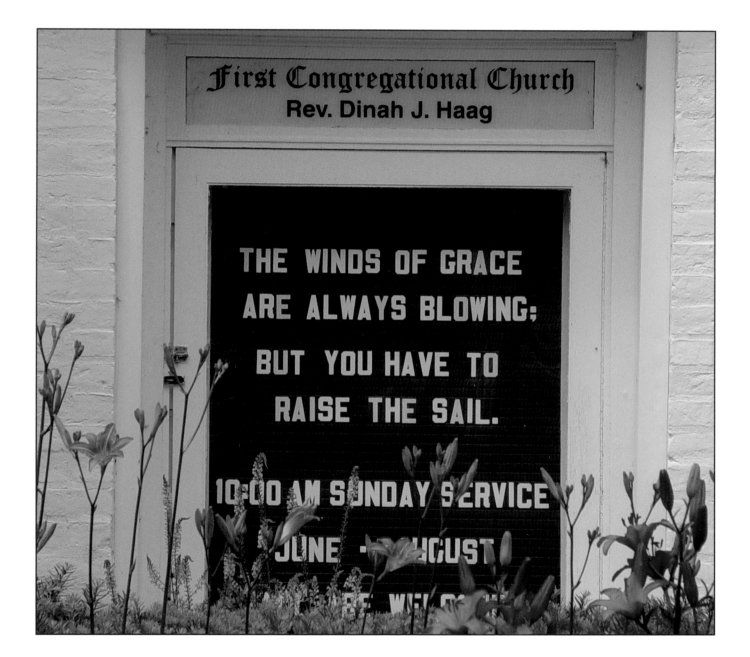

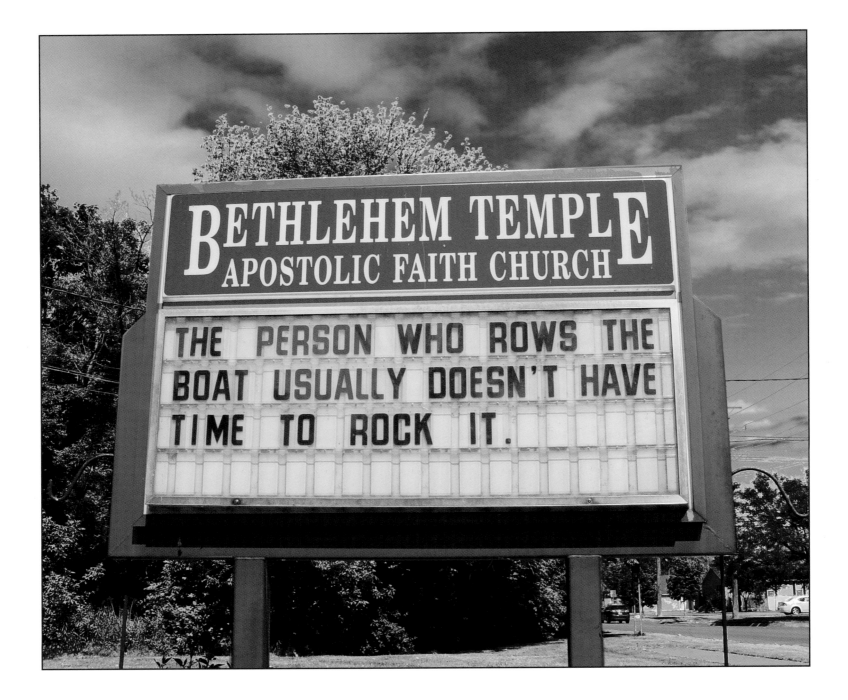

NEW PROSPECT
BAPTIST CHURCH
EVERYONE NEEDS TO BE LOVED
ESPECIALLY WHEN THEY DONT
DESERVE IT

WHAT KINDA CAR?

If Jesus drove the paved city streets and the gravel back roads of America, how would he react to the church signs he saw along the way? Would he be pleased with those marquees that speak of sacrifice, service, and love? Would he laugh or would he wince at those signs that compare his nature with that of a popular soda or detergent?

While the church sign on the opposite page asks us to consider how Jesus would drive, two songwriters ask another road-related theological question: What would Jesus drive?

You see a luxury car's too pretentious
Yeah, and SUVs eat too much gas
All mini-vans and those compact sedans
They just can't go all that fast
As I pondered I came to an answer
'Bout which wheels would fit Him just right
If the Lord came again to live among men
What kinda car would He drive?

He'd drive a pickup truck
Carpenter tools in the back
He'd cruise around in that heaven on wheels
Doin' every kinda kindly act
Choppin' wood for the widow next door
Haulin' goods for the hungry and poor
If you were stuck in a rut, He'd lift you up
In His short-bed, step-side, half-ton pickup truck.

From "What Kinda Car?" © 2005 SME Music (BMI)

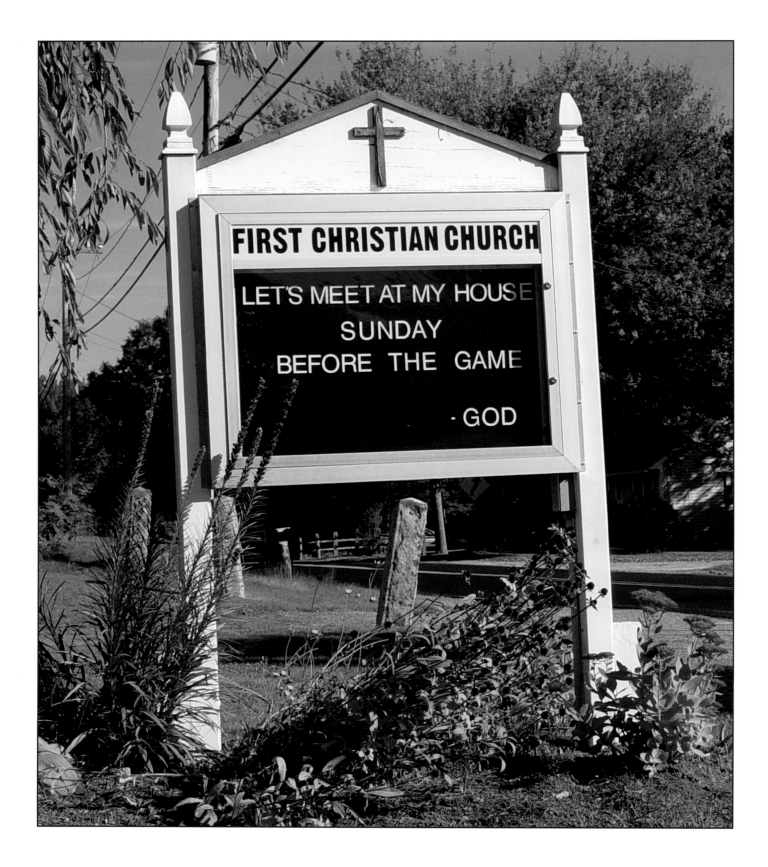

Above: This church lost many of its letters at the hands of vandals one Saturday night. On Sunday, the church issued this amusing appeal for help from the community. Below: Neither strong winds nor heavy rains could wash away the optimism of this church, reminding us to forget our problems and count our blessings.

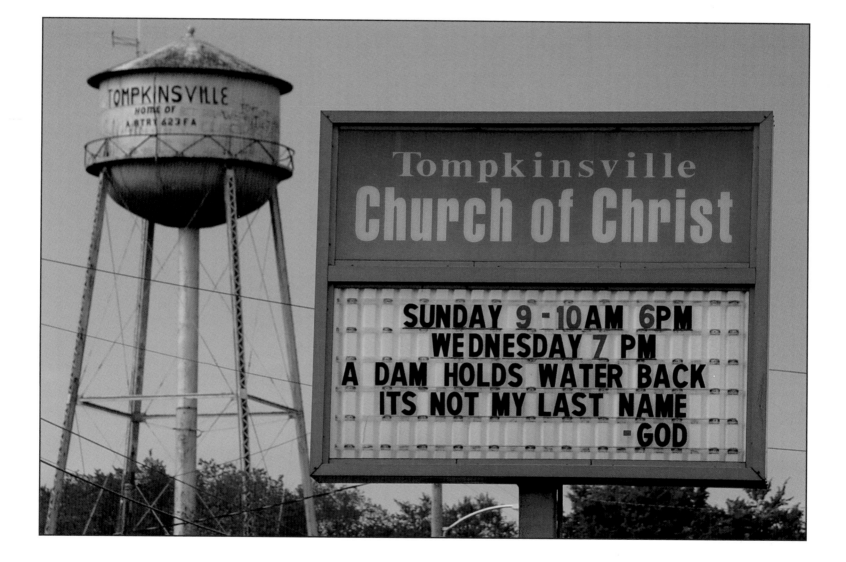

SAY WHAT?

Do church signs ever say what they don't mean to say? You betcha.

Call it irony. Call it bad grammar. Call it the law of unintended consequences. But whenever a sign tries to say too much – as when it refers to both the Sunday sermon and an unrelated church activity – the results can be hilarious or downright baffling.

SERMON: THE REALITY OF HELL COME EARLY AND HEAR OUR CHOIR

IT'S A DOGGONE HEAVENLY WORLD

Do dogs go to heaven? Proud dog owners might give a resounding thumbs (or paws) up. Cat enthusiasts might say — not so much. St. Francis of Assisi, patron saint of animals, would likely suggest that salvation is offered to all of God's creatures.

This contentious debate between the Catholics of Our Lady of Martyrs and the Presbyterians of Beulah became an internet sensation. These images shot back and forth by email umpteen times every dog year. Most people were amused by the wackiness of it all. Others were put off that two churches would go head to head in such a public way. One email I received opined, "The Catholics are displaying a much better sense of humor! You get the impression that the Presbyterians are actually taking this seriously and are getting a bit upset..."

But alas, at the end of the day, it turns out we can't answer the theological question of a doggie afterlife. Nor can we say that Catholics have it over the Presbyterians when it comes to a sense of humor.

You see, unlike all the other photos in this book, the images on the opposite page are not real photos of real church signs. Instead, these pictures were made on a very popular website (www.says-it.com) that allows you to create your own imaginative church signs. (One way to see that these signs are not actual signs in real time? Notice how the cars in the church lot and the light on the church buildings never change.)

So if you want a sign to say:

Dogs Go to Heaven, Cats Go to Purr-gatory!

You can do that with just a few clicks of your, ah, mouse.

FRANKLIN
CHURCH of CHRIST

SUNDAY BIBLE STUDY   9:00 A.M.
SUNDAY WORSHIP   10:00 A.M.
WEDNESDAY BIBLE STUDY   7:00 P.M.

IN TRYING TIMES, DON'T QUIT TRYING

324 FRANKLIN ROAD   •   794-2359

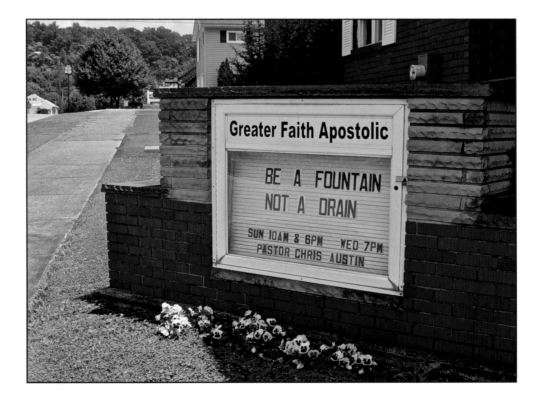

Greater Faith Apostolic

BE A FOUNTAIN
NOT A DRAIN

SUN 10AM & 6PM   WED 7PM
PASTOR CHRIS AUSTIN

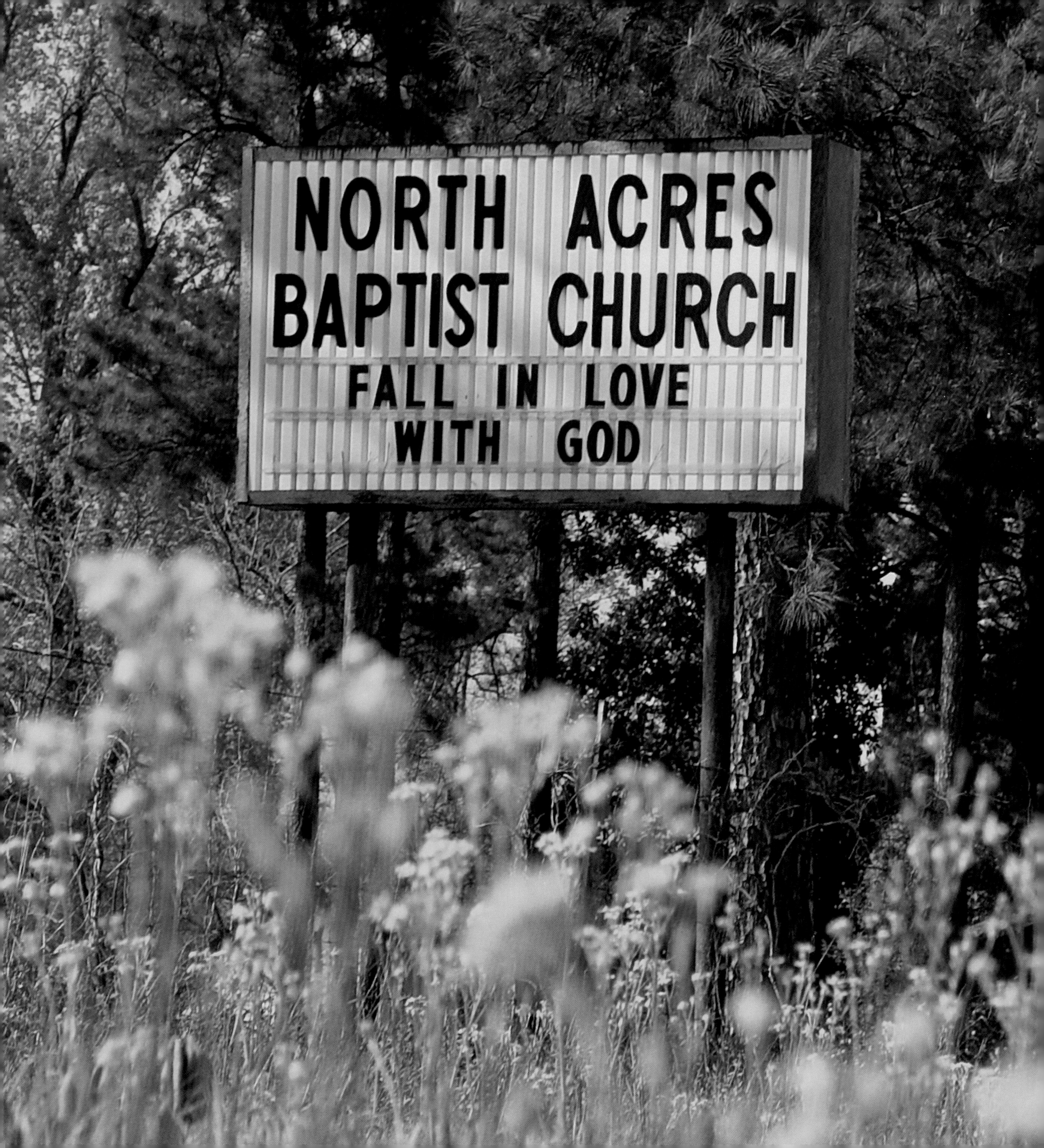
NORTH ACRES
BAPTIST CHURCH
FALL IN LOVE
WITH GOD

ETERNITY

EVERY FLOWER OF
SPRINGTIME SPEAKS
OF THE RESURRECTION

Donated by the Brown Family

WHAT'S IN A NAME?

You can worship in the most likely and unlikely places. In Virginia, you can seek the light in Darkesville. In Oregon, treat yourself to windy sermons at three Boring churches (Nazarene, Baptist, and Orthodox). In Arizona, leave your worries behind at the Carefree Community Church, agreeably located on the Carefree Highway. Let go of your doubts in Uncertain, Texas, at the aptly named Church of the Uncertain. And feel free to engage in some thorny theological debates about salvation at the New Testament Baptist Church in Truth or Consequences, New Mexico.

Just five miles outside a swampy, lowland town in Michigan – said to freeze over every winter – you can take refuge with the Methodists, the Lutherans, and a host of other denominations. But keep in mind, once you leave those sanctuaries and enter Hell (pop. 266), you're on your own.

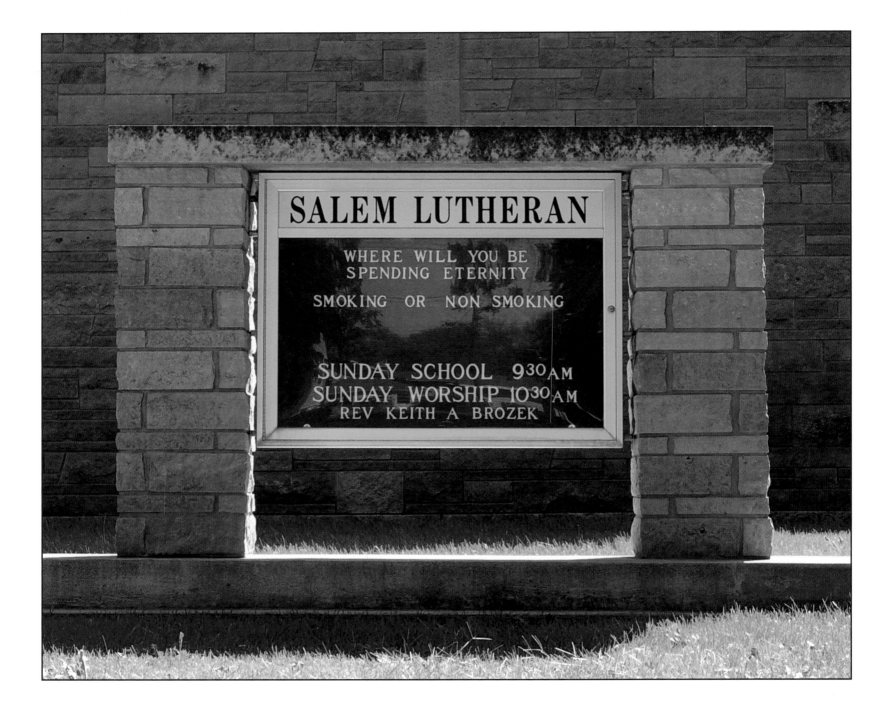

THANKS AND ACKNOWLEDGEMENTS

To Patric Kelly for his hard work, creativity, and unsurpassed skills as a graphic artist — and for giving this book shape, style, and life.

To Ellen Bradbury and the entire team at Lithographics Inc. in Nashville, TN. If you're looking for an American printing company with equipment that's state of the art — and a staff of hardworking professionals with big hearts — then this is the place for you.

To the Greater Pleasant View Baptist Church in Brentwood, TN, whose sign opposite the Contents page inspired the making of this book. And to Doris Richardson for her dedication in making sure the weekly message always touches the minds and spirits of those who pass by.

To the thousands of Pastors who take their work — but not themselves — seriously.

To Pastor Steve Molin at Our Savior's Lutheran Church in Stillwater, MN. Pastor Steve offered the Church Sign Trivia Challenge (p. 33) and is one of the most engaging and inventive church sign scribes. He is the author of *If There Were No Lutherans, Would There Still Be Green Jell-O?* (available at www.churchsignguy.com).

To Pastor Phil Kinzer and The West End Church of Christ in Nashville, TN, whose sign always offers an incredibly rich variety of wit and wisdom. It's the kind of sign that drivers go out of their way to see.

To Reverend Elaine Lush and the welcoming messages at the Goodwood United Church in Ontario, Canada, one of which inspired the illustration on p. 9.

To Reed Galin, for power lunches and powerfully funny conversations, and for the two photos he contributed on p. 46 and p. 109.

To Ryland Sanders, the creator of the church sign generator website, who kindly provided the "All Dogs Go To Heaven" series on p. 118. You can see more faux signs at www.says-it.com.

To Jeff Hinton and Quint Randle, members of the band Joshua Creek, and the two outstanding songwriters of "What Kinda Car?" (p. 101). To hear their music, go to www.joshuacreekmusic.com.

To one study that suggests that 10% of new members are drawn to the church because of the sign out front. And to Lee St. Louis, another imaginative songwriter, who described how one little "misplaced" sign worked wonders in the life of a country church.

The Old Pine Valley Church (The Beer Sign)

This is the story about a little church that just couldn't get anywhere
For there was a tavern across the street, and everyone was going there
Then one day something happened that no one could explain
And for this little church everything had changed

They said the congregation was badly in decline
When it came to serving God, no one had the time
They tried everything they knew but nothing seemed to work
Then someone hung a beer sign on the old Pine Valley Church

Chorus
The day they hung the beer sign on the old Pine Valley Church
They finally got the devil to do the good Lord's work
People came from miles around to celebrate His word
The day they hung the beer sign on the old Pine Valley Church

The town drunk staggered in and said, "I think I"ll have a shot"
The preacher said to him, "My son, faith is all we've got"
But if you have a glass or two I'm sure you'll realize
That just a little trust in God will open up your eyes

No one knew who hung the sign, no one seemed to care
They only knew the chosen few came from everywhere

Repeat Chorus   © 2010 Lee St. Louis

To those signs that speak of perseverance and optimism in the face of great hardship. Like this one seen on Will and Guy's humor website (www.guy-sports.com).

EVENINGS AT 7 IN THE PARISH HALL

Mon.	Alcoholics Anonymous
Tue.	Abused Spouses
Wed.	Eating Disorders
Thu.	Say NO to Drugs
Fri.	Teen Suicide Watch
Sat.	Soup Kitchen

SUNDAY'S SERMON

AMERICA'S JOYOUS FUTURE

To any church thinking about preaching from a sign for the first time, an enjoyable reference book is *Signs For These Times* by Ronald Glusenkamp.

Finally, to all the churches whose signs appear within these pages,
and to the thousands of churches that encourage us with
words of faith, love, and laughter.

CHURCH SIGN LOCATIONS

6	Brentwood, TN
10	West Brattleboro, VT
11	Blythewood, SC
12	Florence, AL
13	Salina, KS
14	Hays, KS
15	Lynchburg, VA
16	Nashville, TN
17	Portsmouth, NH
18	Utica, KY
19	Fayettville, TN
21	Athens, GA
22	San Francisco, CA
23	Council Bluffs, IA
24	Atkins, VA
25	Atkins, VA
26	Lindon, UT
27	St. Louis, MO
28	Tompkinsville, KY
29	Montpelier, VT
30	Sulphur Springs, TX
31	Lancaster, PA
32	Petaluma, CA
34	Mobile, AL
35	Gulf Resort Beach, FL
36	Kauai, HI
37	Muscle Shoals, AL
40	Thomson, GA
41	Vergennes, VT
42	Nashville, TN
43	Santa Monica, CA
44	Russellville, KY
45	Mt. Vernon, KY
46	Arrington, TN
47	Junction City, LA (top)
	Frankfort, MI (bottom)
49	Monroe, LA
50	Cincinnati, OH
51	Kalamazoo, MI (top)
	Terre Haute, IN (bottom)
	Vienna, IL (right)
52	Ft. Collins, CO
53	Collinwood, TN
54	Kinston, AL
55	Manchester, NH
56	Camden, AR
58	Kirkland, AZ
59	Henderson, KY (top)
	Scottsburg, IN (bottom)

60	Evanston, IL
61	Auburn, KY
62	Columbia, TN
63	Nashville, TN
64	Nashville, TN
65	New York, NY
68	Glendora, CA
69	Olivet, TN
70	Auburn, GA
71	Henderson, KY
74	Brentwood, TN
75	Osmond, NE

76	Nashville, TN
77	Salina, KS
78	Eagle Mills, AR
79	Foley, AL
81	Staunton, VA
82	Troy, AL
83	Chattanooga, TN
86	Portland, TN (top)
	Russellville, KY (bottom)
87	Frankfort, MI
88	West Nashville, TN
89	Columbia, TN
90	Lancaster, PA
91	Lancaster, PA

92	Clinton Township, MI
93	Nashville, TN
94	Hadar, NE (top)
	Tyrone, PA (bottom)
95	Springfield, KY
96	Elkton, TN
97	Vega, TX
98	Florence, AL
99	Dubach, LA
100	Monroe, LA
102	Cleveland, OH
103	Nashville, TN
104	Nesser, LA
105	Petaluma, CA
106	Louisville, KY
107	Selma, OR
108	Kittery, ME
109	Brentwood, TN
110	Whittington, LA
111	Reno, NV (top)
	Baton Rouge, LA (bottom)
112	Tompkinsville, KY
113	Tompkinsville, KY
114	Billings, MT
116	Nashville, TN
117	Omaha, NE
118	Everywhere/Nowhere
120	Austin, TX
121	Franklin, TN (top)
	Ironton, OH (bottom)
122	Pine Bluff, AR
123	Magnolia, AR
126	Wytheville, VA
127	Alexandria, LA
128	Winona, MS
129	Terre Haute, IN
130	Bellevue, TN
131	Paint Lick, KY
132	West Monroe, LA
133	Livingston, MT
134	Brent, AL
136	Stromsburg, NE
137	Wytheville, VA
138	Atlanta, IN
139	East Nashville, TN
140	Elizabethtown, KY
141	Jessup, GA
144	Brentwood, TN